D1529805

DISCARD

CELEBRITIES
GIVING BACK

Kayleen
Reusser

Mitchell Lane
PUBLISHERS

P.O. Box 196
Hockessin, DE 19707
www.mitchelllane.com

Ways to Help After a Natural Disaster
Ways to Help Children With Disabilities
Ways to Help Chronically Ill Children
Ways to Help Disadvantaged Youth
Ways to Help in Your Community
Ways to Help the Elderly
Volunteering in Your School
Celebrities Giving Back

Copyright © 2011 by Mitchell Lane Publishers

All rights reserved. No part of this book may be reproduced without written permission from the publisher. Printed and bound in the United States of America.

Library of Congress
Cataloging-in-Publication Data

Reusser, Kayleen.
 Celebrities giving back / by Kayleen Reusser.
   p. cm. — (How to help)
 Includes bibliographical references and index.
 ISBN 978-1-58415-922-3 (library bound)
 1. Charities—United States—Case studies. 2. Philanthropists—United States—Case studies. 3. Celebrities—United States—Case studies. I. Title.
 HV91.R48 2011
 361.7'4092273—dc22

                                        2010014904

Printing   1   2   3   4   5   6   7   8   9

                                              PLB

CONTENTS

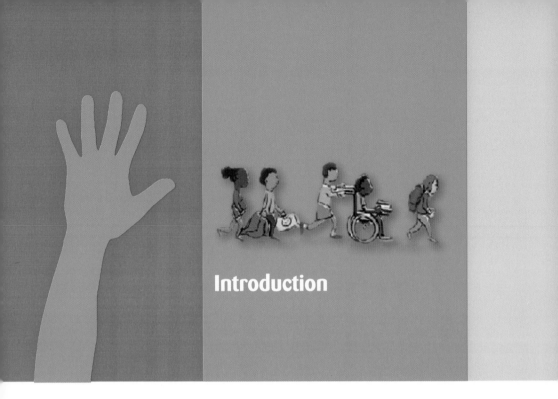

Introduction

Can anyone really make a difference?

Throughout history, people who have accomplished the most have understood that real change occurs at the simplest thresholds of life. One moment. One deed. One relationship.

Consider these sayings by famous people:

"Whatever you do may seem insignificant, but it is most important that you do it." —Gandhi

"The pen is mightier than the sword." —19th-century English novelist Edward Bulwer-Lytton

"To sin by silence when they should protest makes cowards of men." —Abraham Lincoln

"How far that little candle throws his beams! So shines a good deed . . ." —William Shakespeare

"You gain strength, courage and confidence by every experience in which you really stop to look fear in the face. . . . You must do the thing you think you cannot do." —Eleanor Roosevelt

These people—some of the most influential who ever lived—knew the power that could be found in investing their efforts in others.

In 2005, world leaders met at the World Economic Forum to discuss poverty (left to right): Bill Clinton (U.S.), Bill Gates (U.S.), Thabo Mbeki (South Africa), Tony Blair (UK), Bono (UK), and Olusegun Obasanjo (Nigeria).

Many famous entertainers also realize the value of giving back to their communities. In this book, you will read about actors, musicians, politicians, and athletes. One man dreamed of building a hospital and decided on its location after reading a newspaper article. Another teen formed a computer business and went on to become one of the world's richest men. Today, he uses his knowledge of technology to save lives around the world.

The purpose of this book is to encourage you to think about how you can help others. You may not have money to build a hospital, but you could help deliver flowers to people who are ill, bringing armloads of cheer to patients.

Do you like to draw? Create get-well cards for people in nursing homes. Love to read? Arrange a 30-minute reading session for preschoolers at your local library. Keep your eyes and ears open for opportunities to volunteer. No matter where you live, opportunities to volunteer abound.

When you volunteer, you meet people with different backgrounds and perspectives. Those experiences can help you to understand yourself, and to find your strengths and weaknesses.

Find volunteer opportunities in your community, then get permission from your parents or guardians to get involved. You'll be glad you did!

Bono

Bono, singer of the Irish rock group U2, has been fighting poverty and hunger around the world for more than two decades. His involvement in Africa began shortly after he performed with U2 at the Live Aid concert in London in 1985. The concert was a fund-raiser for famine relief in Africa.

In 1986, Bono visited Ethiopia, where he saw hundreds of hungry children. When he later visited Nicaragua and El Salvador, he witnessed similarly sad situations. "Two and a half million Africans are going to die next year because they can't get drugs that we take for granted," Bono said during his Heart of America tour in 2002. "That's not a cause. That's an emergency."[1]

Since then, Bono has dedicated his life to helping children around the world lead better lives. "Everybody wants to make an impact with their life," he said, "whether it's small scale . . . or on a grand scale, in changing their communities and beyond. I just want to realize my potential."[2] As part of his quest to help the world's starving people, Bono created several programs to address poverty.

The goal of ONE is to persuade the U.S. government to give funds to fight AIDS and poverty around the world, particularly in Africa. Since Bono founded the organization in 2005, it has grown to more than two million members.[3]

Recognizing the American public's love for shopping, Bono created an organization called (RED). Through it, retailers set aside a percentage of their profits for research on AIDS, tuberculosis, and malaria.

The effects of (RED) on raising funds to fight poverty are well known. At an art auction in New York City in 2008, Bono's (RED) charity attracted many celebrities who supported his cause. By the end of the evening, more than $42 million had been bid to benefit the Global Fund of the United Nations Foundation, which works to fight AIDS in Africa.

During his travels to fight poverty, Bono talks with people affected by HIV/AIDS, including this 14-year-old boy from Tanzania who lost both of his parents to the disease.

Bono was especially pleased with the night's highest-priced item. A painting of a medicine cabinet from British artist Damien Hirst, called *Where There's a Will, There's a Way*, sold for $7.15 million. "Damien Hirst's medicine cabinet is so striking because he's made pills a centerpiece of his work for years," Bono said. "And now the idea that these pills have gone from being a work of art to providing real pills for people who will die without them is very poetic to me."[4]

By 2009, sales of (RED) products such as T-shirts, sunglasses, coffee, and computers had raised enough funds to provide a year's worth of medication for 825,000 Africans diagnosed with AIDS.[5]

A third member of Bono's charitable organizations, EDUN, is a clothing company with factories in Africa, South America, and India. Bono created the company in 2005 to increase jobs in those places. "Africans we met during our trips . . . said what they wanted more than anything was a job," Bono wrote on his blog.[6]

Bono's music often reflects his humanitarian concerns. During the Heart of America tour, Bono wrote these words to "American Prayer":

Besides offering financial help, Bono cheers African children diagnosed with HIV/AIDS – sometimes by dancing with them!

"These are the hands/What are we gonna build with them?/This is the church you can't see/Give me your tired, your poor and huddled masses/All are yearning to breathe free/American prayer, (This is my) American prayer."[7]

Bono explains why he wrote the song: "My prayer is that this country, which has unparalleled economic, technological, military, and cultural power, will rethink its purpose that made it great. Millions of lives hang in the balance in parts of the world that depend on decisions made a long way from them."[8]

For his efforts to help people around the world, Bono was knighted by the Queen of England. He has also received three nominations for the Nobel Peace Prize.

EDUN
http://www.edunonline.com/
ONE
http://www.one.org/us/
(RED)
http://www.joinred.com/

Nancy Brinker, right, and her sister, Susan G. Komen

Nancy Brinker

In the early 1980s, Nancy Brinker made a promise to her dying sister, Susan G. Komen. She would educate people about ways to fight breast cancer—the disease that eventually took Susan's life—and offer support to survivors. Brinker has done so through an organization she founded in 1982 called Susan G. Komen for the Cure (formerly Susan G. Komen Breast Cancer Foundation).

By emphasizing the importance of medical exams, research, and support among survivors, the Susan G. Komen for the Cure group has changed the way the world thinks about breast cancer. In 1982, the federal government devoted $30 million to breast cancer research, treatment, and prevention; the five-year survival rate for breast cancer, if caught early, was 74 percent. By 2010, the federal government had increased spending to $900 million a year. Better yet, the five-year survival rate was 98 percent.[1]

Part of the money for breast cancer research is generated through the Susan G. Komen Race for the Cure. Brinker founded this group in 1983. Over one million volunteers have participated since 2005, making it the world's largest and most successful education and fund-raising event for breast cancer.[2]

Brinker is concerned about educating women in America and around the world about breast cancer, particularly about the need for early detection. In an article for *Newsweek*, she wrote, "We've come a long way in America toward improving attitudes and treatment [for breast cancer]. The same must now happen beyond our borders."[3]

Brinker is not content to see this illness linger. "We are so close to creating a world without breast cancer," she said. "The science is there. Now is the time for us to see this fight through so that no one ever has to fear breast cancer again."[4]

Susan G. Komen for the Cure
5005 LBJ Freeway, Suite 250
Dallas, TX 75244
1-877-GO KOMEN (1-877-465-6636)
http://ww5.komen.org/

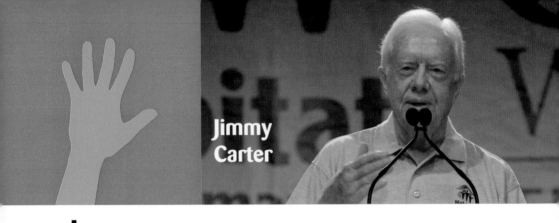

Jimmy
Carter

In 1976, Millard and Linda Fuller of Americus, Georgia, and a group of friends tried to think of a way to solve the problem of homelessness. The Fullers wanted to help financially disadvantaged families live in safe, adequate housing. They knew the answer was not to simply give new homes to the families. That would not create a sense of ownership. The answer was to bring together a group of future homeowners who would work with volunteers to build the homes. The Fullers called their organization Habitat for Humanity International.

In the 30 years since Habitat for Humanity began, volunteers have constructed more than 350,000 houses around the world. More than 1.75 million people in 3,000 communities live in adequate, safe housing they might not otherwise have been able to afford. This practice reflects Habitat's mission statement: "What the poor need is not charity but capital, not caseworkers but co-workers. It is not a handout."[1]

Jimmy Carter, who was U.S. president from 1977 to 1981, and his wife, Rosalynn, have been involved with Habitat for Humanity International for many years. In 1984 they led a work group to New York City to help renovate a six-story building. Jimmy Carter had always enjoyed carpentry work (the White House staff gave him tools for his workshop when he left the presidency). That experience planted the seed for the Jimmy and Rosalynn Carter Work Project (formerly the Carter Work Project).

The Carters supervise the building of homes around the world. During one interview about his involvement with Habitat, Carter responded to a humorous question: "Did you ever envision becoming so prolific a builder of latrines?"

Carter laughed, then replied, "In Ethiopia . . . we taught people how to build very simple latrines. Women have adopted building them as a kind of liberation movement—there had been a rigid taboo against a woman relieving herself in the daytime—so although we thought we'd have about 10,000 latrines, we've passed 340,000. Now

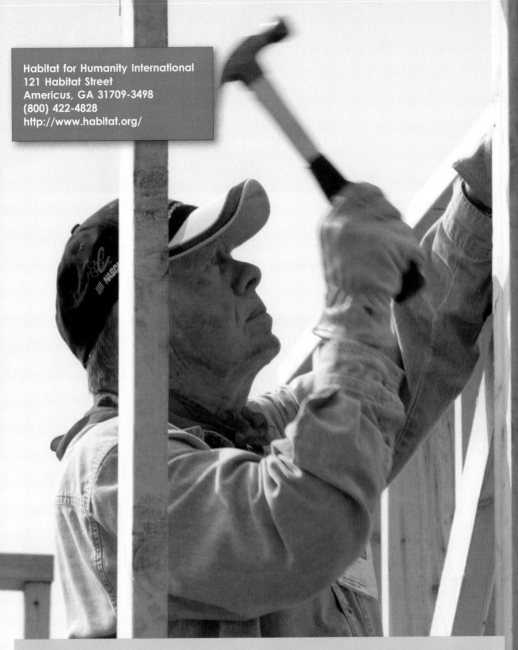

Habitat for Humanity International
121 Habitat Street
Americus, GA 31709-3498
(800) 422-4828
http://www.habitat.org/

instead of my being famous for negotiating peace between Israel and Egypt, I'm famous in Ethiopia for being the No. 1 latrine builder."[2]

In their 80s, the Carters have continued to work one week each year with Habitat for Humanity. Jimmy Carter says, "Habitat has opened opportunities for me to cross the chasm that separates those of us who are free, safe, and financially secure . . . from our neighbors who enjoy few, if any, of these advantages of life."[3]

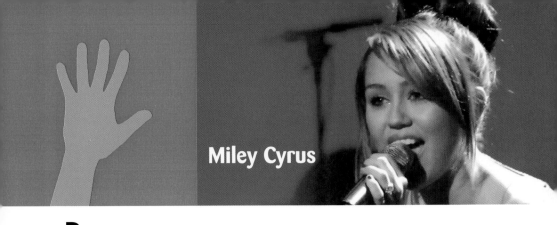

Miley Cyrus

Before popular entertainer Miley Cyrus moved to California to begin her show *Hannah Montana,* her mother, Tish, said, "Honey, if you're going to do this, it would really make sense to use it to bring awareness to kids your age that you really can help others."[1]

Since then, Miley Cyrus has given her time and talents to a number of charities. For Mother's Day 2008, she and Tish donated to the Libby Ross Foundation. This organization, founded in 1999 by Lori Ross and Marla Willner, promotes early detection of breast cancer, research to eradicate the disease, and support programs for patients.

The Cyrus women, along with other celebrity mothers and daughters, decorated yoga bags with jewels for an auction on eBay's charity site. The goal was to raise funds for the charity's yoga program designed for women with breast cancer.

Cyrus has also contributed her musical talents to support City of Hope in Los Angeles, California. The hospital is dedicated to treating and preventing cancer and other diseases. In 2007, she donated $1 from every ticket sold for her Best of Both Worlds concert tour to cancer research at City of Hope. The concert series raised more than $1 million.[2] Cyrus has also supported City of Hope by visiting its pediatric cancer patients with her father, Billy Ray Cyrus.

Another organization Cyrus helps with is Musicians on Call. This charity brings live and recorded music to patients' bedsides, which promotes healing for patients, families, and caregivers. This organization has chapters in New York, Philadelphia, Nashville, and Miami.

City of Hope
1500 East Duarte Road
Duarte, CA 91010
(626) 256-4673
http://www.cityofhope.org/

Libby Ross Foundation
1710 First Avenue #226
New York, NY 10128
(212) 831-9592
http://www.thelibbyrossfoundation.com/

Musicians on Call
1133 Broadway, Suite 630
New York, NY 10010-8072
(212) 741-2709
http://www.musiciansoncall.org/

Boomer Esiason with his son, Gunnar

Boomer Esiason

Boomer Esiason was used to working hard on the football field. He set 17 school records for passing and total offense during an All-American career at the University of Maryland. He led his college team to the Citrus Bowl in 1983.

Esiason began playing for the National Football League in 1984 when the Cincinnati Bengals drafted him. While playing for the Bengals, he was selected as the NFL Most Valuable Player. Later, he played for the New York Jets and the Arizona Cardinals.

Esiason was a quarterback for the Jets in 1993 when he learned that his young son, Gunnar, was afflicted with cystic fibrosis. Using the same grit and determination he had shown as a professional athlete, Esiason organized a program to help his son and others diagnosed with cystic fibrosis. It is called the Boomer Esiason Foundation.

Cystic fibrosis affects more than 30,000 Americans, most of whom are diagnosed by the age of two. This genetic disorder causes the body to produce unusually thick, sticky mucus that clogs the lungs and obstructs the pancreas. This, in turn, keeps the body from breaking down and absorbing food.

Among the ways the Boomer Esiason Foundation helps cystic fibrosis patients is to award money to families for travel and relocation costs when cystic fibrosis patients need lung transplants. The organization also offers college scholarships to people with cystic fibrosis. The money offered by the foundation comes from donations by businesses and individuals. Esiason encourages people to raise donations by conducting golf outings, football games, and elegant dinners. Volunteers staff the events, so all the proceeds go directly to the foundation.

As a teen, Gunnar has been able to play football with his high school team at Friends Academy in Melville, New York. He is determined to live life fully. "I've been at every one of these games," he said. He has either played on the field or served as a ball boy. "To finally play

Boomer Esiason visits patients in Miami Children's Hospital Dan Marino Center. He presented the center with a $25,000 check from FedEx, an NFL sponsor.

in it, I can't even describe what it's like," he added. "I'm still kind of caught up in the moment."[1]

Years earlier, when Gunnar was learning how to play football (he has played soccer and lacrosse as well), Boomer expressed optimism about people who live with cystic fibrosis. "You wouldn't know Gunnar has the disease. I honestly believe these kids have a future."[2]

Boomer Esiason Foundation
483 10th Avenue, Suite 300
New York, NY 10018
(646) 292-7930
http://esiason.org/

Doug Flutie

Doug Flutie Sr. has never taken success for granted. In 1984, while playing for Boston College, he made one of the most famous quarterback plays in college football history: he completed a 48-yard touchdown pass just as the game ended. Because of that amazing throw, Flutie's team beat Miami 47-45. For his efforts that day and throughout the season, Flutie was awarded the prestigious Heisman Trophy, recognizing him as the most outstanding college football player of that year.

After college, Flutie played in the Canadian Football League for eight years, then with the National Football League's Buffalo Bills. In 1999, he set the Bills' team record for rushing yards by a quarterback. Flutie later played with the New England Patriots before retiring in 2006. In 2007, he was inducted into the College Football Hall of Fame. After his retirement, he began working as a college football analyst for ESPN and ABC Sports.

That hard work ethic and physical stamina helped Flutie organize the Doug Flutie Jr. Foundation for Autism. The program is named after his son. Dougie was diagnosed with autism in 1995. (The Fluties also have a daughter, Alexa.)

Autism is a disorder that affects the brain's normal development of social and communication skills. It affects individuals differently, and there is a "spectrum" of behaviors associated with it. According to the Centers for Disease Control and Prevention, approximately 1.5 million Americans live with autism spectrum disorder, with 1 in every 150 American children exhibiting autistic tendencies. Most of them are boys. There is no known cause or cure for autism.[1]

Doug Flutie with his son, Doug Jr.

15

With his income as a professional athlete, Doug Flutie Sr. and his wife, Laurie, could afford to purchase the expensive equipment that Dougie needed, such as a special stroller that cost $2,000. The Fluties knew that many families with autistic children could not afford such expenses. Their concern for other families with autistic members inspired them to form the foundation.[2]

The Doug Flutie Jr. Foundation for Autism promotes awareness of and support for families affected by autism spectrum disorders. It awards grants to nonprofit organizations that provide services for children with autism and to organizations that conduct research on the causes and effects of autism. By 2010, the Fluties had awarded $10 million in grants to programs and to families with members who have autism.[3] It had also distributed 350 computers to families of children with autism and their school districts.

The grant money comes from donations, fund-raisers, and endorsement promotions featuring Doug and Doug Jr. Each year Doug Flutie Sr. supports various fund-raising events for the foundation, including the Doug Flutie Jr. Celebrity Golf Classic, an all-star basketball tournament, and a 5K road race. A breakfast cereal, Flutie Flakes, has also helped to raise money for the foundation.

The Fluties know Dougie will probably never throw a football or tie his shoes, but they have chosen to look on the bright side. "My whole career, every place I've been, I've had to start over," said Doug Flutie Sr. "It was the same situation with Dougie. For a while you're going through the Why, why, why? but then it's, Okay— what do I do now?"[4]

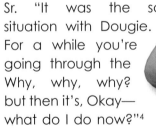

The Doug Flutie Jr. Foundation for Autism
P.O. Box 767
Framingham, MA 01701
1-866-3AUTISM
(508) 270-8855
http://www.dougflutiejrfoundation.org/

Bill and Melinda Gates

As a teenager, Bill Gates loved to work with computers. In the 1970s, computers were large, heavy, and expensive. Most businesses had one, but computers were not user-friendly. Despite these obstacles, Bill envisioned an America in which every home owned a computer.

Gates was a whiz at programming computers—writing special languages that computers understood to process information. While still in high school, he created his own computer business. In 1975 he and a friend founded Microsoft Corporation. This business paved the way for smaller, personal computers to be built at prices families could afford. As a result of his hard work and knowledge, Gates became one of the world's richest men.

Beginning in 1994, Bill and his wife, Melinda, who live in the Seattle area, began giving away millions of dollars to fund charitable programs around the world. Great believers in libraries as sources of information, in 1998 they donated $20 million to the Seattle Public Library.[1] They also gave $20 million to the Massachusetts Institute of Technology to build a laboratory for its computer science program,[2] and $100 million to help children around the world receive life-saving vaccines.[3]

In 2000 they organized the Bill and Melinda Gates Foundation. The purpose of the organization was to award money to programs that emphasized improving global health, education, and libraries. Some of the money they have given away includes $145 million to help prevent the transmission of AIDS around the world.

By 2001, the couple had endowed more than $21 billion for philanthropic causes. Part of this included $750 million to help launch the Global Fund for Children's Vaccines, $50 million to help the World Health Organization's efforts to eradicate polio, and $3 million to help prevent the spread of AIDS among young people in South Africa. In December 2005, the Bill and Melinda Gates Foundation announced it would disburse $84 million to Save the Children and a program to fight infant mortality in developing countries.

The generosity of Bill and Melinda Gates spurred other people to action. One of the biggest supporters has been American billionaire businessman Warren Buffett, who pledged to give several billion dollars to the foundation. In 2005, Bill and Melinda Gates and U2 singer Bono were named *Time* magazine's Persons of the Year for their charitable work toward reducing poverty and disease throughout the world.

There seemed to be no end to the money Bill and Melinda wanted to distribute to the world's people in need. In 2006, their foundation increased its spending on eradicating the disease of tuberculosis from $300 million to $900 million. They also donated $75 million to funding development of a pneumonia vaccine, as well as donating $150 million to improving agriculture in Africa.

As a result of the support and influence of the Bill and Melinda Gates Foundation, payments in 2008 for programs promoting education and health in the United States and around the world totaled $2.8 billion.[4]

In July 2008, Bill Gates resigned his position as manager of Microsoft to spend more time working on the Bill and Melinda Gates Foundation. He admitted he finds working for the foundation to be as intriguing as developing a company like Microsoft. "These are intense, complex issues. . . . Bringing top people together, taking risks, feeling like something very dramatic can come out of it—that's something the previous work and the work now have in common,"[5] Gates said. He also added, "I think all billionaires should give away the vast majority of their fortunes—though I don't say they shouldn't leave anything to their kids. I think they would enjoy it, their kids would be better off, and the world would be better off. I'm a great believer that great wealth should go from the richest to the poorest."[6]

Bill and Melinda Gates Foundation
P.O. Box 23350
Seattle, WA 98102
(206) 709-3100
http://www.gatesfoundation.org/

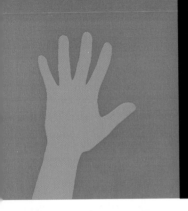

Tony Hawk

When Tony Hawk was given a skateboard at age nine, no one could have predicted how that piece of equipment would affect his life. Over the next few years, he perfected his athletic skills with the board. By age 16, Tony had won enough skateboarding competitions to qualify him as the best skateboarder in the world. More important, at the skate park, he found friends and an outlet for exercise and self-expression.[1]

During the 1980s and early 1990s, Hawk became the face of skateboarding, especially when he completed the first 900 in 1999. The 900 is an aerial spin on a skateboard, rotating 2½ times and then landing on the board upright. Hawk's fame increased when a series of video games featuring his unique moves was released.

Twenty years after Hawk received his first skateboard, the sport had gained more than 13 million participants in the United States. Unfortunately, many city leaders lacked funds to provide at-risk youth with skate parks. By 2010, only an estimated 3,000 skate parks were available in the United States.[2] Lacking suitable places to practice, most skaters rode wherever they could, including streets and parking lots. This tended to create ill will with neighborhood and community leaders.

In 2002, Hawk organized the Tony Hawk Foundation, which encourages the construction of skate parks in towns and cities across the country. "It doesn't take long for cities to realize their modest skate parks get more use than the local tennis courts or baseball fields," he says.[3]

The organization offers financial and social support to skateboarders in mostly underprivileged neighborhoods. By awarding grants totaling more than $2.7 million, the foundation has helped establish 427 skate parks across the United States. "Our money doesn't build an entire park, but it gives the kind of push some parks need to get it approved or get more funding," Hawk said in an interview in 2009. "I think our endorsement goes a long way."[4]

Tony Hawk performs daring stunts on his skateboard at fund-raisers, including one for the Elizabeth Glaser Pediatric AIDS Foundation in California.

Tony Hawk Foundation
1611-A S. Melrose Drive #360
Vista, CA 92081
(760) 477-2479
http://www.tonyhawkfoundation.org/

Hawk helps communities design skate parks. When he attends grand openings for the parks, his excitement is obvious. "It's rewarding to see joy on the faces of kids who realize their years of perseverance have finally paid off," he says. "The appreciation of local skaters is overwhelming."[5]

Angelina Jolie and Brad Pitt

Actors Angelina Jolie and Brad Pitt met while starring in the 2005 film *Mr. and Mrs. Smith*. Previously, they had each helped poor people in developing countries. Jolie had traveled to refugee camps around the world, including Africa, Pakistan, and Cambodia. In 2003 she was appointed Goodwill Ambassador for the United Nations High Commissioner for Refugees (UNHCR).

In 2004, Pitt traveled to South Africa and Ethiopia to call attention to the AIDS epidemic in those countries. "I've spent a wonderful week traveling this beautiful continent," he said, "listening to the people and learning about the AIDS crisis, the extreme poverty and what people in America can do to help."[1]

After they started dating in 2006, Jolie and Pitt combined their interests in humanitarian causes to establish the Jolie-Pitt Foundation. They donated $1 million to the charities Doctors Without Borders and Global Action for Children. They also gave $1 million to refugees in Pakistan, and programs for the African countries of Chad and Darfur. By the end of 2006, Jolie and Pitt had donated more than $8 million to charities.[2]

Jolie was so moved by the poverty in Cambodia that she adopted a small boy from that country, naming him Maddox. She then created the Maddox Jolie-Pitt (MJP) Foundation. The organization's multiple projects focus on improving some of the worst problems in Cambodia: alleviating poverty, providing children with education, protecting the environment, establishing health care, and empowering women.[3]

Despite juggling busy acting schedules and parenting six children (three biological and three adopted), Jolie and Pitt have not slowed in seeking to serve the world's poor people. In the United States, Pitt launched an affordable housing project in the impoverished Lower Ninth Ward of New Orleans—one of the neighborhoods hit worst by 2005's Hurricane Katrina. "We will have 100 homes and it will be the greenest, most intelligently designed neighborhood in the United

People of the SOS Children's Village in Amman, Jordan, were overjoyed to visit with United Nations Goodwill Ambassador Angelina Jolie and American actor Brad Pitt.

States," he said. "We have families . . . whose electric bills are $8, $12. It's a big deal for anyone, but for a low-income family, it's life-changing."[4]

In October 2009, Pitt and Jolie traveled to Syria and Jordan on a United Nations Goodwill visit to displaced Iraqi civilians. They also went to Haiti, one of the world's poorest countries, to help with projects sponsored by the Yéle Haiti Foundation. This organization, founded by Grammy Award–winning musician Wyclef Jean in 2005, distributes food and mobilizes emergency relief.

In an interview about her trip to Afghanistan to provide assistance to people in need, Jolie gave an answer that perhaps sums up the motivation behind her and Pitt's involvement with the world's poor. "Behind the labels—refugees, internally displaced persons, asylum seekers—are people with the same hopes, fears, sorrow and happiness as anyone," she said. "Their life experiences are often deeply tragic but also uplifting."[5]

MJP Foundation
Group #02, Rumchek4 village
Rotanak commune
Battambang district and province
Kingdom of Cambodia
(855) 53 730 171
http://www.mjpasia.org/

Doctors Without Borders
http://www.doctorswithoutborders.org/

Global Action for Children
http://www.globalactionforchildren.org/

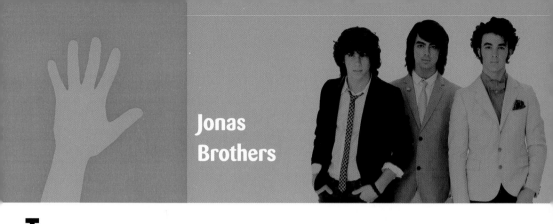

Jonas Brothers

The Jonas Brothers—Kevin, Joe, and Nick—got their start in 2005 when Columbia Records signed them as a band. Their first album, self-titled and released in 2007, and 2008's *A Little Bit Longer* were both certified platinum. Since then, the brothers have released *Lines, Vines, and Trying Times,* toured worldwide, and starred in hit movies.

Despite being nominated for a Grammy and selling 8 million albums, the Jonas Brothers have refused to let their musical careers run their lives. Finding time to help other people is a priority for them. The brothers started the Change for the Children Foundation with a donation of $1 million to help children facing adversity related to health issues. "Kids can have a tough time growing up, overcoming obstacles in their lives and achieving their full potential, especially when their health is holding them back," said Nick Jonas, who was diagnosed with type 1 diabetes at the age of 13. "We wanted to let them know that despite major problems like cancer, they can succeed."[1] Some of the programs the foundation supports include the American Diabetes Association's Diabetes Camp and St. Jude Children's Research Hospital in Memphis.

Over the years the brothers have developed individual interests. Joe ran a race in 2009 in support of the Special Olympics in San Antonio, Texas.[2] Nick testified in 2009 at a Congressional hearing to request federal funding for diabetes research in support of the Juvenile Diabetes Research Foundation.[3] And Kevin supports volunteerism.

The Jonas Brothers often work with other celebrities to help charities. In fall 2008, they, along with Miley Cyrus and actress/singer Demi Lovato, helped raise $1.2 million at a sold-out concert to benefit cancer research and treatment at City of Hope.[4] This organization, located in Duarte, California, is a leading research and treatment center for cancer, diabetes, and other life-threatening diseases. The money raised at the concert would support clinical trials of potential

When the Jonas Brothers played in a charity softball event in July 2009, they raised $2,900 for their Change for the Children Foundation.

new treatments for type 1 diabetes. More than 700,000 Americans have this form of diabetes.[5]

The brothers developed a volunteer text program to encourage other people to help in their communities. By texting JONAS to 30644 and entering their ZIP code, people living anywhere in the United States can receive notice of two volunteer opportunities each month.[6]

As Nick Jonas discovered, people who need help can be as close as your own neighborhood. After visiting a Dallas food bank close to his home in January 2010, he donated $25,000 to replenish its shelves. "Volunteering or giving a financial gift is something I can do to help," he said.[7]

Change for the Children
http://www.changeforthechildren.org/

City of Hope
(see page 12)

Peyton Manning

Whenever someone enters the children's section of St. Vincent Hospital in Indianapolis, they think of Peyton Manning, quarterback for the city's football team, the Colts. They don't think of him for his ability to throw a football or because he was the Super Bowl XLI MVP. They think of him because the children's hospital bears his name: Peyton Manning Children's Hospital at St. Vincent. On September 6, 2007, the children's hospital was renamed in appreciation of Manning's devotion to the children of Indianapolis and other cities across the nation.[1]

In 1999, Manning established the PeyBack Foundation to help disadvantaged children in Louisiana, Tennessee, and Indiana. The foundation provides assistance to organizations such as Boys and Girls Clubs; area food banks; and summer, after-school, and youth athletic programs. By 2010, it had donated more than $3.6 million to those organizations.[2]

One of the agencies the PeyBack Foundation assists in Indianapolis, the East Tenth United Methodist Children and Youth Center, offers meals, child-care services, and tutoring to economically disadvantaged children. The center charges parents of its students only a fraction of what it costs to care for them. The rest is made up through donations, a significant portion of which comes from the PeyBack Foundation.

In addition to financial assistance, the center regularly receives invitations from Manning for its 100 students to attend a Colts game during the season as his guests. In addition, each Christmas season, Manning takes over the Children's Museum of Indianapolis for the PeyBack Holiday Celebration. More than 1,000 children from 100 community agencies attend. The special event includes dinner, a visit from Santa, special Christmas gifts from Peyton, and the opportunity to visit the nationally renowned museum. The foundation also hosts Christmas parties in New Orleans and Knoxville, Tennessee.

"Peyton Manning is such an example of someone who cares," said Casmir Hill, director of East Tenth United Methodist Children and Youth Center. "He's a great role model for the kids. And when they see him in person, oh, it's such a huge deal."[3]

Since 2003, Manning has hosted the PeyBack Bowl. Each year he and other Indianapolis Colts coaches and players form bowling leagues to raise money for underprivileged children in Indianapolis. Over the years, the PeyBack Bowl has raised more than $985,000.[4]

An opportunity to play in the arena for the New Orleans Saints when he was a high school football player was an experience Peyton Manning never forgot. He created the same experience for Indianapolis area athletes with the PeyBack Classic, launched in 2000. "I wanted Indianapolis high school teams to feel that same sense of pride that I had when I ran onto that field with my teammates," he said. "I also wanted a chance to pay back local high school athletic programs for providing such wonderful opportunities to these kids."[5]

Peyton's Pals, another program of the PeyBack Foundation, sponsors a series of monthly educational, cultural, and community service events for 20 middle school kids. Students learn about living a healthy lifestyle and how to deal with peer, family, and school pressures.

Peyton Manning's generous spirit touches more than students in Indianapolis. In 2005, he and his brother Eli, who plays for the New York Giants, organized a plane full of relief supplies to be delivered to Hurricane Katrina victims in Baton Rouge, Louisiana. That year, Peyton Manning was named the Walter Payton NFL Man of the Year for his off-the-field community service.

Why does Peyton Manning give so much of his time and money to helping kids? "I figured I had great parents, a great support system and just a blessed childhood," he said. (His father, Archie Manning, was a quarterback for the New Orleans Saints.) "What can I do to help kids have some of those same opportunities? Provide them with some of the same type of support, and give them opportunities to have memorable moments in their lives."[6]

PeyBack Foundation
6325 N. Guilford, Suite 201
Indianapolis, IN 46220
(877) 873-9225
http://www.peytonmanning.com/

Barack and Michelle Obama

A desire to spur U.S. citizens to volunteer prompted President Barack Obama in June 2009 to organize a program called United We Serve. He and his wife, Michelle, gave speeches and performed many acts of service to promote the program. "This summer, the President and I are asking you to make time and do your part," said Michelle Obama, "wherever your interests lie, whether it's working with young people or caring for the sick and elderly in our hospitals, or helping to make the homes in your neighborhood more energy efficient or any other issue. The most important thing is for you to get involved."[1]

The President and First Lady helped Congressional family members and others pack 15,000 backpacks with books, healthy snacks, and other items for U.S. military children.[2]

"America faces the greatest challenges it has seen in generations," President Obama said. "Instead of creating a new government bureaucracy, we need to build on the extraordinary efforts taking place in communities throughout the country. Michelle and I are proud to participate . . . today with so many Congressional families and nonprofit organizations."[3]

The President proclaimed September 11, 2009, as Patriot Day and National Day of Service and Remembrance. He also approved Congress' request that September 11—the anniversary of the 2001 terrorist attacks on the United States—be recognized annually as a National Day of Service and Remembrance.

During his speech, the President said, "Working together, we can usher in a new era in which volunteering and more service is a way of life for all Americans. Deriving strength from tragedy, we can write the next great chapter in our nation's history and ensure that future generations continue to enjoy the promise of America."[4]

United We Serve
http://www.serve.gov/

Paul Newman, Richard Petty, and the Victory Junction Gang

Question: What do you get when you mix salad dressing, an actor, and a racecar driver?

Answer: Victory Junction, a camp for children with chronic medical conditions or serious illnesses.

The idea for a camp for chronically ill children began in the early 1980s when Paul Newman began selling his homemade salad dressing, popcorn, salsa, spaghetti sauce, and lemonade in supermarkets around the country. Newman, one of the biggest stars in Hollywood, designated the profits from Newman's Own foods to the construction of a camp for children with serious illnesses. He called it The Hole in the Wall Gang Camp, naming it for the group of outlaws he led in one of his most popular movies, *Butch Cassidy and the Sundance Kid.*

In 1988, Newman opened the first Hole in the Wall Gang Camp in Ashford, Connecticut. Children with cancer and serious blood disorders who were too ill to attend regular camps could attend Newman's camp at no charge. Since 2004, other Hole in the Wall Gang Camps have been built in New York, California, Florida, Ireland, and France.

The idea for Victory Junction occurred in 1999 when Kyle and Pattie Petty and their son, Adam, participated in a charity motorcycle ride for Camp Boggy Creek in Florida. The camp was a member of Newman's Association of Hole in the Wall Camps.

Kyle Petty is a member of the Petty family of racecar drivers. He is also a philanthropist. Since it began in 1995, the annual Chick-fil-A Kyle Petty Charity Ride Across America has donated $9 million to worthy organizations.[1]

Sadly, Adam Petty was killed in a racecar crash in 2000. Kyle and Pattie decided to do something in Adam's memory. After Adam had seen Camp Boggy Creek, he dreamed of building a camp in North Carolina for children with serious illnesses. Pattie and Kyle knew the

Paul Newman, Richard Petty, and the Victory Junction Gang

American actor Paul Newman prepares to take a camper fishing at one of his Hole in the Wall Camp locations.

best thing they could do to remember Adam was make his dream a reality with Victory Junction.

Victory Junction is located on 84 acres near Randleman, North Carolina. The land was donated by Kyle Petty's father, legendary racer Richard "The King" Petty. The camp has a racecar theme, with buildings appropriately named: Adam's Race Shop, Goody's Body Shop (medical center), Hendrick Motorsports Fuel Stop (dining hall), Silver Theater, Kyle Petty Charity Ride Across America Water Park, and Jessie's Horse Power Garage (stables and riding arena). The camp is open for 10 weeks in the summer and 19 weekends in the spring and

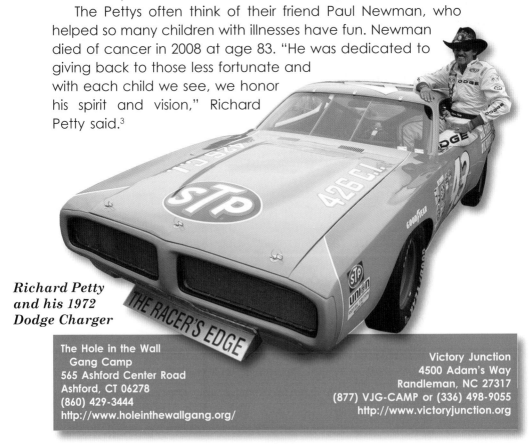

fall. It offers fishing, water sports, horseback riding, miniature golf, crafts, and bowling.

The first campers entered Victory Junction in June 2004. Within five years, 7,000 children from 47 states and three countries had attended Victory Junction at no charge. The campers had been diagnosed with such illnesses as cancer, burns, heart disease, AIDS, asthma, sickle cell anemia, epilepsy, hemophilia, immune system deficiencies/HIV, spina bifida, kidney disease, liver disease, cystic fibrosis, diabetes, and autism.[2] At Victory Junction, they could minimize their illness and focus on fun.

As the camp is located on the East Coast, the Pettys realized many children from the Midwest and Western United States could not attend. They planned to build a second Victory Junction, this one in Kansas City, Kansas. It was scheduled to open in 2010.

The Pettys often think of their friend Paul Newman, who helped so many children with illnesses have fun. Newman died of cancer in 2008 at age 83. "He was dedicated to giving back to those less fortunate and with each child we see, we honor his spirit and vision," Richard Petty said.[3]

Richard Petty and his 1972 Dodge Charger

The Hole in the Wall
  Gang Camp
565 Ashford Center Road
Ashford, CT 06278
(860) 429-3444
http://www.holeinthewallgang.org/

Victory Junction
4500 Adam's Way
Randleman, NC 27317
(877) VJG-CAMP or (336) 498-9055
http://www.victoryjunction.org

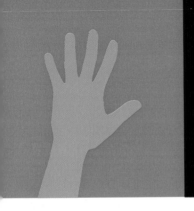

Rihanna

When Grammy Award–winning singer Rihanna was growing up on the island of Barbados, she knew what she wanted to do when she grew up. She says, "When I was young and I would watch television and I would see all the children suffering, I always said, 'When I grow up, I want to help.' "[1]

In 2006, Rihanna created the Believe Foundation to assist terminally ill and disadvantaged children around the world. The foundation helps financially disadvantaged children by providing funds for medical bills, school supplies, and clothing.

Rihanna has performed a number of concerts to raise funds for her foundation. After many performances, she has met disadvantaged children, signing autographs and posing for pictures with them. "Not long after I was in the position where I could help, I started to visit all these children's hospitals," she says. "I have a soft spot for kids. I just want to help and make sure they are happy."[2]

In addition to the Believe Foundation, Rihanna's commitment to helping children has included becoming a 2007 Cartier Love Charity Bracelet Ambassador. A portion of each sale of the jewelry was given to the Believe Foundation.

She also performed at Madonna's Raising Malawi/UNICEF fund-raiser, and she sang at the Justin Timberlake Shriners Open golf tournament in 2008 in Las Vegas. Proceeds benefited Shriners Hospitals for Children.

Rihanna is determined to reach as many children in need as possible. "As a kid, the thing I hated most was disappointment, so I never want to disappoint kids," she says. "I always want to put a smile on their faces. Kids are the future."[3]

The Believe Foundation
c/o Berdon LLP
360 Madison Avenue, 9th Floor
New York, NY 10017
http://www.believerihanna.com/

When pop singer Shakira was eight years old, she and her father walked past a park near their home in Colombia, South America. They saw many children wearing ragged clothing and looking hungry. Shakira's family had recently suffered hard times—her father's jewelry business had gone bankrupt and the family had to sell their cars and other luxury items. Shakira felt sorry for herself until she saw the children in the park and how they had nothing, not even a family. "Despite our situation, my parents wanted me to know that it could be far worse," she recalls. She promised herself that if she was ever able to help people less fortunate, she would.[1]

Her first major album, called *Pies Descalzos* ("Barefoot" in Spanish), was named for the children she had seen that day in the park. "I hoped that, in some small way, I was able to give a voice to those children whom no one seemed to listen to or care about," she said.[2]

Believing education was the key to a better world for everyone, Shakira founded Pies Descalzos in Colombia when she was only 18 years old. Schools that are funded by her foundation offer children nutritious meals, quality education, and counseling services for those who have experienced tragedies.

In 2008, Shakira expanded the school program with a similar U.S.-based nonprofit organization called Barefoot Foundation. The organization consists of support programs for children and their families.

In an article for *Newsweek* magazine, Shakira wrote, "Globally, 72 million children don't attend primary school and another 226 million aren't in secondary school. In addition, hundreds of millions of children attend some inadequate version of school but can't access the type of quality education that they really need to succeed."[3]

In between tours and recording music (she has sold over 50 million albums worldwide), Shakira meets with world leaders to discuss how to address the problems she sees as plaguing children today:

In Haiti, Shakira's foundation is working with Architecture for Humanity to build a school and provide education, school meals, clean water, and sanitation services.

expensive school fees, under-qualified teachers, and the high cost of textbooks and meals in schools. "[Government leaders] must decide that a child's poverty is not an excuse," she says. "The leaders must educate all children regardless of what family or neighborhood they are born into. And they must prioritize education funding [in their budgets]."[4]

Shakira can still close her eyes and imagine the faces of the homeless children who lived in her neighborhood when she was a little girl. She remembers their hopeless expressions, and she knew many sniffed glue or took drugs to forget the hunger and the cold.

"But I have also seen how education can alter the course of a child's life forever . . . ," she adds. "It's amazing how much difference each person can make."[5]

Barefoot Foundation
Attn: Global Philanthropy Group
1500 4th Avenue, Suite 600
Seattle, WA 98101
http://www.barefootfoundation.com/

Danny and Marlo Thomas

In the 1950s, when Hollywood actor Danny Thomas decided to build a hospital for children, he thought about locating it in Boston. The city was close to Harvard and other prestigious universities that could help with research to find cures for such diseases as cancer.

Then Thomas read a newspaper article. The story told of an eight-year-old African-American boy in the South who was hit by a car. The boy was seriously injured, but emergency rooms would not treat him because of his race. This neglect cost the boy his life.

Thomas's heart ached for the little boy. He had already decided his new hospital would offer affordable, accessible health care to every patient. Thomas decided the best place for the new hospital would be Memphis, Tennessee. He named the hospital after St. Jude, the patron saint of desperate causes.[1]

St. Jude Children's Research Hospital opened its doors in 1962. Since then, it has grown to treat more than 5,500 seriously ill children each year. One of its triumphs is a cure rate of 90 percent for cases of acute lymphoblastic leukemia—the most common childhood cancer.

"We know so much more today about the individual characteristics of a child's cancer, including its genetic structure, so we can personalize the treatment," said Marlo Thomas, Danny's daughter. Marlo serves as National Outreach Director for the hospital. After Danny passed away in 1991, Marlo assumed her father's position as St. Jude's principal fund-raiser, work she continues today.

"St. Jude researchers discovered leukemia can be treated without the use of radiation, which is a toxic approach," she said. "By using personalized chemotherapy regimens, our researchers have improved cure rates for the disease and that's why doctors across the country refer their young patients to us."[2]

Marlo Thomas followed her father's journey into acting, nabbing the lead role in the popular 1960s TV show *That Girl*. Over the course of her long acting career, Marlo has received a Grammy Award, four Emmys, a Golden Globe, and the Ellis Island Medal of Honor for exceptional humanitarian efforts and outstanding contributions to the United States. She now attends events around the country to promote St. Jude to corporations, individual donors, and other celebrities. She, her brother Tony, and her sister Terre host the annual Runway for Life Celebrity Fashion Show in Hollywood, which raises $1 million a year for the hospital.[3]

Danny Thomas would no doubt have been pleased about his family's continued involvement in St. Jude's welfare. He would also have been happy to know that the hospital continues to offer free health care to its patients. It absorbs not only costs not covered by medical insurance, but also travel, food, and lodging for patients and their families.

Marlo Thomas understands her father's devotion to St. Jude. "When you attend the high school graduation or wedding of a child who was supposed to die—well, it's irresistible," she says. "It motivates me to continue to work."[4]

Actress Marlo Thomas works tirelessly to solicit donations for St. Jude Children's Research Hospital, which her father Danny Thomas helped to found in 1962.

St. Jude Children's Research Hospital
262 Danny Thomas Place
Memphis, TN 38105
(901) 595-3300
http://www.stjude.org

Oprah Winfrey

"One of the things I've learned is that the best way to enhance your own life is to contribute to somebody else's." —Oprah Winfrey[1]

Born in Mississippi to a single mother, TV talk show host Oprah Winfrey spent most of her childhood with little stability, living first with her grandparents in Mississippi and then moving to Wisconsin with her mother. When that arrangement proved unsatisfactory, the teenager moved to Tennessee to live with her father. With his loving discipline and enforcement of education, Oprah's life changed for the better. "I believe my own success has come from the gift of learning," she said.[2]

Upon entering college, Oprah found a job as a news anchor. In 1984, realizing that covering hard news was not her niche, she accepted a job as host for *AM Chicago*, a television talk show. This type of job seemed as natural to Oprah as breathing. Her friendly personality and interest in people instantly turned it into a hit. Soon, *The Oprah Winfrey Show* was broadcast from television stations in more than 120 U.S. cities.

It seemed there was nothing that Oprah, the Queen of Talk, could not do. She acted in prizewinning films, started a production company, and purchased a magazine she named *O: The Oprah Magazine*.

As her media empire grew, so did her concern for children. In 1991, Oprah proposed federal child protection legislation designed to keep national records on convicted child abusers. In 1993, President Bill Clinton signed the national "Oprah Bill" into law. The bill guaranteed strict sentencing of individuals convicted of child abuse.

In 1998, Oprah started a charity called Oprah's Angel Network. This charity raised approximately $80 million for educational and community projects in more than a dozen countries. In 2005 it helped 1,000 families affected by Hurricane Katrina in Texas, Mississippi, Louisiana, and Alabama. Inspired by Oprah's Book Club, which introduces people to contemporary quality literature, the network provided books for children around the world, including China and St. Petersburg, Russia. Through the Use Your Life Award, it recognized

Since Oprah Winfrey opened a leadership academy for girls in South Africa in 2007, the $40-million school has offered free tuition, books, and housing to 450 students annually. She announced that in 2011, she would shift her focus from her Angel Network to the Oprah Winfrey Leadership Academy Foundation, which supports the school.

50 U.S. organizations that had impacted the lives of others. The Use Your Life Award built more than 55 schools in 12 countries, providing education for thousands of children in rural areas throughout the world, including areas in China and South Africa.[3]

Oprah pledged $10 million to Nelson Mandela to build a school for girls in South Africa. "I know that this Academy will change the trajectory of these girls' lives," she said. "They will excel and pass their excellence on to their families, their nation, and our world."[4]

For her efforts in helping others, Oprah has been honored with a number of awards, including the Global Leadership Award from the United Nations. She was also named one of *Time* magazine's Most Influential People, and she was given the first Bob Hope Humanitarian Award at the Emmy Awards.

Oprah Winfrey Leadership Academy Foundation
http://oprahwinfreyleadershipacademy.
o-philanthropy.org/

CHAPTER NOTES

Bono
1. Cathleen Falsani and Mark Allan Powell, "Bono's American Prayer," *Christianity Today,* March 1, 2003, http://www.christianitytoday. com/ct/2003/march/2.38.html?start=1
2. Ibid.
3. ONE: About ONE Members. http://www.one. org/us/about/ourmembers.html
4. Brian Orloff and Jeffrey Slonim, "Bono AIDS Charity Auction Raises $42 Million," *People,* February 15, 2008, http://www.people.com/ people/article/0,,20178398,00.html
5. David Yonke, "Bono Taps into Buying Power: U2 Singer's Projects for Africa Studied in Academia," *The [Toledo, Ohio] Blade,* September 12, 2009, http://www.allbusiness. com/society-social-assistance-lifestyle/social- justice/12924154-1.html
6. Virginia Simmons, "A Few Words From Bono," *ONE Blog,* October 13, 2006, http://action.one. org/blog/?p=195
7. Falsani and Powell.
8. Ibid.

Nancy Brinker
1. Susan G. Komen for the Cure: About Us: "Our Work," http://ww5.komen.org/AboutUs/ OurWork.html
2. Susan G. Komen for the Cure: "Participate in an Event," http://ww5.komen.org/findarace. aspx
3. Nancy Brinker, "Debating Mammograms," *Newsweek,* Vol. 154, Issue 25, December 12, 2009, http://www.newsweek.com/id/226427
4. Mark Newman, "MLB Continues Fight Against Breast Cancer," *MLB.com,* May 7, 2009, http://mlb.mlb.com/news/article. jsp?ymd=20090507&content_ id=4617366&vkey=news_mlb&c_id=mlb

Jimmy Carter
1. Habitat for Humanity fact sheet, Frequently Asked Questions, http://www.habitat.org/how/ factsheet.aspx
2. Carolyn Kaster, "10 Questions for Jimmy Carter," *Time,* September 25, 2007, http://www. time.com/time/arts/article/0,8599,1665544,00. html
3. "Jimmy Carter and Habitat for Humanity," http://www.habitat.org/how/carter.aspx

Miley Cyrus
1. "Miley Gives Back," *People, Miley Cyrus Special Issue,* Vol. 70, August 6, 2008, http:// www.people.com/people/archive/ article/0,,20221834,00.html
2. "The Walt Disney Company Is Presenting Miley Cyrus, Jonas Brothers and Demi Lovato in a Special Concert to Benefit City of Hope on September 14," City of Hope Press Release, August 11, 2008, http://www.cityofhope.org/ about/publications/news/Pages/walt-disney- company-presenting-miley-cyrus-jonas-brothers- demi-lovato-in-a-special-concert-to-benefit- city-of-hope-sept-14.aspx

Boomer Esiason
1. Bob Herzog, "Gunnar Esiason Has Always Risen to Challenge," *Newsday,* June 24, 2009.
2. "Esiason Brings $1M to Cystic Fibrosis Fund," *USA Today,* August 22, 2002.

Doug Flutie
1. Autism Society, "About Autism," http://www. autism-society.org/site/PageServer?pagename=a bout_home
2. Welcome to the Doug Flutie Jr. Foundation for Autism, http://www.dougflutiejrfoundation.org/
3. The Doug Flutie Jr. Foundation for Autism, "History," http://www.flutiefoundation.org/About- The-Foundation-History.asp
4. Karl Taro Greenfeld, "The Homecoming," *Sports Illustrated,* Vol. 103, Issue 14, October 10, 2005.

Bill and Melinda Gates
1. Seattle Public Libraries, "Seattle Public Library Receives Largest Ever Private Gift: $20 Million Gift from Bill and Melinda Gates Kicks Off Capital Campaign," November 24, 1998. http://www.spl. org/lfa/lfapr/gatesgift.html
2. William Gates III, "Software Breakthroughs: Solving the Toughest Problems in Computer Science," video, February 26, 2004. http://mitworld.mit.edu/ video/209
3. Bill and Melinda Gates Foundation: "Foundation Timeline and History," http://www. gatesfoundation.org/about/Pages/foundation- timeline.aspx
4. Bill and Melinda Gates Foundation: "Foundation Fact Sheet," http://www.gatesfoundation.org/ about/Pages/foundation-fact-sheet.aspx
5. Maria Bartiromo, "Melinda and Bill Gates on Making a Difference," *BusinessWeek,* February 5, 2009, http://www.businessweek.com/magazine/ content/09_07/b4119021540910.htm
6. John Acher, " 'Give It Away, You'll Enjoy It,' Gates Tells Rich," Reuters, June 3, 2009, http:// www.reuters.com/article/idUSTRE55253F20090603

Tony Hawk
1. Tony Hawk Official Website: Biography, http://www.tonyhawk.com/bio.html
2. Tony Hawk Foundation: Background, http://www. tonyhawkfoundation.org/about/background/
3. Tony Hawk Foundation: "Letter from Tony," http:// www.tonyhawkfoundation.org/about/
4. Brandon Schatsiek, "Nederland Skate Park Opens with Help from Tony Hawk: Skateboarding Legend Visits New Facility," *Daily Camera* (Boulder, CO), May 31, 2009.
5. Tony Hawk Foundation: "Letter from Tony," http:// www.tonyhawkfoundation.org/about/

Angelina Jolie and Brad Pitt
1. Brad Pitt Biography, *People.com,* http://www. people.com/people/brad_pitt/ biography/0,,20004328_20,00.html
2. Martyn Palmer, "Brad Pitt: The Man Behind the Soap Opera," *The Times* (United Kingdom), August 1, 2009, http://entertainment.timesonline. co.uk/tol/arts_and_entertainment/film/ article6728806.ece?token=null&offset=0&page=1

3. MJP Foundation: http://www.mjpasia.org/
4. Palmer.
5. Adrian Edmondson, "Actress, Pin-up and Earth Mother. But There's Another Angelina Who Dives into Hellholes," *The Sunday Times,* November 9, 2008.

Jonas Brothers
1. Laura Kim, "Jonas Brothers Back Diabetes Research at City of Hope," City of Hope Press Release, May 28, 2009, http://www.cityofhope. org/about/publications/eHope/2009-vol-8-num-5-may-28/Pages/jonas-brothers-back-diabetes-research-at-city-of-hope.aspx
2. Change for the Children Foundation: "Joe Jonas Runs Like a Champion," http://www. changeforthechildren.org/view_article. php?id=745
3. Change for the Children Foundation: "Nick Jonas Testifies for Diabetes Research Funding at Children's Congress in Washington, DC," http://www.changeforthechildren.org/view_ article.php?id=193
4. Kim.
5. Ibid.
6. Change for the Children Foundation: "Jonas Brothers Volunteer Text Program," http://www. changeforthechildren.org/view_article. php?id=89
7. Diane Jennings, "Teen Heartthrob Nick Jonas Offers Time, Cash to Food Bank," *The Dallas Morning News,* January 3, 2010. http://www. dallasnews.com/sharedcontent/dws/news/ localnews/stories/010310dnmetjonas.449dc24. html

Peyton Manning
1. Peyton Manning Children's Hospital at St. Vincent, http://www.peytonmanning.com/ Pages/Main/PMCH/PMCH.htm
2. Peyton's Peyback Foundation, http://www. peytonmanning.com/
3. Jarrett Bell, "Hospital Renaming Crowns Manning's Charity Efforts," *USA Today,* September 5, 2007, http://www.usatoday.com/ sports/football/nfl/colts/2007-09-05-manning-hospital_N.htm
4. Melanie Heaviland, "2009 PeyBack Bowl a Huge Success!" Article Archived: August 26, 2009, http://www.peytonmanning.com/pages/ main/displayarticle.asp?article=826200943204
5. Peyton Manning's Peyback Classic, http:// www.peytonmanning.com/Pages/Main/ PeyBack/PeyBackClassic/Classic_Home.htm
6. Bell.

Barack and Michelle Obama
1. "First Lady Michelle Obama, Cabinet Members Kick Off United We Serve," National and Community Service Press Release, June 22, 2009, http://www.nationalservice.gov/about/ newsroom/releases_detail.asp?tbl_pr_id=1382
2. "President Obama and the First Lady Pack 15,000 Backpacks for Children of Our Troops," National and Community Service Video, June 25, 2009, http://www.nationalservice.gov/ about/newsroom/releases_detail.asp?tbl_pr_ id=1405

3. Ibid.
4. Barack Obama, "Patriot Day and National Day of Service and Remembrance 2009," National and Community Service Press Release, September 10, 2009, http://www. nationalservice.gov/about/newsroom/releases_ detail.asp?tbl_pr_id=1507

Paul Newman, Richard Petty, and the Victory Junction Gang
1. Kaley Lyon, "Riding with Purpose," *The Hays Daily News,* May 13, 2009, http://www. allbusiness.com/sports-recreation/sports-games-outdoor-recreation-auto/12454441-1.html
2. Victory Junction: Current Partners, http://www. victoryjunction.org/partners/current_partners. php
3. "Paul Newman's Passion Was Auto Racing," *Foxnews.com,* September 28, 2008, http:// www.foxnews.com/story/0,2933,429242,00.html

Rihanna
1. Stephen M. Silverman, "Rihanna Touring for Kids in Need," *People,* March 27, 2008. http://www.people.com/people/ article/0,,20186594,00.html
2. Ibid.
3. Ibid.

Shakira
1. Shakira, "Education, the Song of Hope," *Newsweek,* Vol. 152, Issue 15, October 13, 2008, http://www.newsweek.com/id/162264
2. Ibid.
3. Ibid.
4. Ibid.
5. Shakira: Philanthropy, "Letter from Shakira," http://www.shakira.com/philanthropy/

Danny and Marlo Thomas
1. Dennis McCafferty, "4 Questions for Marlo Thomas," November 22, 2009, *USAWeekend. com,* http://www.usaweekend.com/apps/ pbcs.dll/article?AID=200991118003
2. Ibid.
3. Stephen Henderson, "The Torchbearer," *Town & Country,* Vol. 161, June 2007.
4. Ibid.

Oprah Winfrey
1. Oprah's Duke University 2009 Graduation Commencement Speech, May 10, 2009, http://www.oprah.com/world/Oprahs-Duke-University-2009-Graduation-Commencement-Speech
2. Jayne Keedle, *Oprah* (Pleasantville, NY: Gareth Stevens Publishing, 2009), p. 6.
3. Oprah's Angel Network Fact Sheet, June 24, 2008, http://www.oprah.com/pressroom/ About-Oprahs-Angel-Network
4. "Oprah Winfrey Leadership Academy for Girls—South Africa Celebrates Its Official Opening," Press Release, January 2, 2007, http://oprahwinfreyleadershipacademy.o-philanthropy.org/academy_opening_200701. pdf

National Organizations

1-800-Volunteer.org
  http://www.1-800-volunteer.org
Alzheimer's Association
  http://www.alz.org/
American Cancer Society
  http://www.cancer.org
American Diabetes Association
  http://www.diabetes.org
AmeriCorps
  http://www.americorps.gov/
Arthritis Foundation
  http://www.arthritis.org/
Boys and Girls Clubs of America
  http://www.bgca.org/
Boy Scouts of America
  http://scouting.org/
Catholic Charities USA
  http://www.catholiccharitiesusa.org/
Charity Vault
  http://www.charity-charities.org/index.htm
Charity Watch
  http://www.charitywatch.org/toprated.html
Children Incorporated
  http://www.children-inc.org
Citizen Corps
  http://www.citizencorps.gov/
Communities in Schools
  http://communitiesinschools.org/
Corporation for National and Community
  Service
  http://www.nationalservice.gov/
Cross-Cultural Solutions
  http://www.crossculturalsolutions.org
Do Something.org
  http://www.dosomething.org
eBay Giving Works
  http://www.givingworks.ebay.com
Family Guide to Volunteering: Zoom into
  Action
  http://www-tc.pbskids.org/zoom/grownups/
  action/pdfs/volunteer_guide.pdf
Feeding America
  http://feedingamerica.org
Feed the Children
  http://www.feedthechildren.org
Food for the Hungry
  http://www.fh.org/
Gifts in Kind
  http://www.giftsinkind.org/
Girl Scouts of America
  http://girlscouts.org
Give Spot
  http://www.givespot.com/donate/food.htm
Goodwill Industries International
  http://www.goodwill.org/
HandsOn Network
  http://vop.handsonnetwork.org/

Humane Society of the United States
  http://www.humanesociety.org/
Idealist Kids and Teens
  http://www.idealist.org/kt/
Junior Red Cross
  Division of the American Red Cross
  http://www.redcross.org
Kids Care Club
  http://www.kidscare.org/
Learn and Serve America
  http://www.learnandserve.gov/
Little Brothers/Friends of the Elderly
  http://www.littlebrothers.org/
Make-A-Wish Foundation of America
  http://www.wish.org/
Meals on Wheels Association of America
  http://www.mowaa.org/
National Audubon Society
  http://www.audubon.org/
National Conference on Volunteering and
  Service
  http://www.volunteeringandservice.org/
National Crime Prevention Council
  http://www.ncpc.org/
National Youth Leadership Council
  http://www.nylc.org/
Peace Corps
  http://www.peacecorps.gov/
Planet Aid
  http://www.planetaid.org/
Planet Protectors Club
  http://www.epa.gov/osw/education/kids/
  planetprotectors/index.htm
Salvation Amy USA
  http://www.salvationarmyusa.org/
Save the Children
  http://www.savethechildren.org
Senior Corps
  http://www.seniorcorps.gov/
Special Olympics International
  http://www.specialolympics.org/
Students Against Drunk Driving
  http://www.sadd.org/
Trees Forever
  http://www.treesforever.org/
U.S. Department of Housing and Urban
  Development Volunteering Site
  http://portal.hud.gov/portal/page/portal/
  HUD/topics/volunteering
U.S. Forest Service
  http://www.fs.fed.us/
U.S. National Park Service
  http://www.nps.gov/index.htm
United Way
  http://www.liveunited.org/
USA Freedom Corps for Kids
  http://www.volunteerkids.gov/

Volunteer Animals
   http://animals.com/collection/Volunteer
Volunteer.gov
   http://volunteer.gov/gov/
Volunteering in America
   http://www.volunteeringinamerica.gov/
Volunteer Jobs
   http://www.groovejob.com/
Volunteer Match
   http://www.volunteermatch.org/
Volunteers for Prosperity
   http://www.volunteersforprosperity.gov/
Volunteers of America
   http://www.voa.org/
VT Seva: Volunteering Together for Service
   http://www.vtsworld.org/
YMCA
   http://www.ymca.net/
Youth Service America
   http://www.ysa.org/
Youth Venture
   http://www.genv.net/
Youth Volunteer Corps of America
   http://www.yvca.org/
YWCA USA
   http://www.ywca.org/

Alabama
Alabama Baptist Children's Homes
P.O. Box 361767
Birmingham, AL 35236
(205) 982-1112
(888) 720-8805 (Toll-free)
http://www.abchome.org/

Manna House Food Distribution Center
2300 Memorial Parkway
Huntsville, AL 35801
http://www.therockfwc.org/extensions/
   manna-house.html

Alaska
Ascent Russian Orphan Aid Foundation
P.O. Box 1305
Palmer, AK 99645
(415) 367-3500
http://www.iorphan.org

Thread Alaska
3350 Commercial Drive, Suite 203
Anchorage, AK 99501
(800) 278-3723
http://www.threadalaska.org/

Arizona
Candlelighter's Weekend Family Retreat
P.O. Box 42436
Tucson, AZ 85733
(520) 777-4911
http://www.candlelightersaz.org

Duet: Partners in Health and Aging
555 West Glendale Avenue
Phoenix, AZ 85021
(602) 274-5022
http://www.centerdoar.org/

Arkansas
Arkansas Children's Hospital
1 Children's Way
Little Rock, AR 72202
(501) 364-1100
http://www.archildrens.org

Northwest Arkansas Children's Shelter
7702 SW Regional Airport Blvd.
Bentonville, AR 72712
(479) 795-2417
http://www.nwacs.com/

California
California Children's Hospital Association
1215 K Street, Suite 1930
Sacramento, CA 95814
(916) 552-7111
http://www.ccha.org

Homeless Children's Network
3265 17th Street, Suite 404
San Francisco, CA 94110
(415) 437-3990
http://www.hcnkids.org/

Tuolumne Trails
22988 Ferretti Road
Groveland, CA 95321
(800) 678-5102
http://www.tuolumnetrails.org/

Colorado
Camp Wapiyapi
910 16th Street, Suite 226
Denver, CO 80202
(303) 534-0883
http://www.wapiyapi.org

The Children's Hospital
13123 East 16th Avenue
Aurora, CO 80045
(720) 777-1234
http://www.thechildrenshospital.org

Connecticut
Connecticut Children's Medical Center
282 Washington Street
Hartford, CT 06106
(860) 545-9000
http://www.connecticutchildrens.org

Delaware
Delaware Foundation Reaching Citizens
640 Plaza Drive
Four Seasons Center
Newark, DE 19702
(302) 454-2730
http://www.dfrcfoundation.org/

Florida
Boggy Creek Camp
30500 Brantley Branch Road
Eustis, FL 32736
(352) 483-4200
http://www.boggycreek.org

Miami Children's Hospital
3100 SW 62nd Avenue
Miami, Florida 33155
(305) 666-6511
http://www.mch.com

Georgia
Camp Sunshine
1850 Clairmont Road
Decatur, GA 30033-3405
(404) 325-7979
http://www.mycampsunshine.com

Hawaii
Parents and Children Together
1485 Linapuni Street, Suite 105
Honolulu, HI 96819
(808) 847-3285
http://www.pacthawaii.org/

Idaho
The Children's Village, Inc.
1350 W Hanley Avenue
Coeur d'Alene, ID 83815
(208) 667-1189
http://www.thechildrensvillage.org/

Illinois
Autism Society of America
Central Illinois Chapter
P.O. Box 8781
Springfield, IL 62791-8781
(217) 241-2023
http://www.asacic.org/

Camp Quality
P.O. Box 641
Lansing, IL 60438-0641
(708) 895-8311
http://www.campqualityillinois.net

Indiana
Little Red Door Cancer Agency
1801 North Meridian Street
Indianapolis, IN 46202-1411
(317) 925-5595
http://www.littlereddoor.org

Iowa
Camp Courageous
12007 190th Street
Monticello, IA 52310-0418
(319) 465-5916
http://www.campcourageous.org/

The Heart Connection Children's Cancer Programs
1221 Center Street, Suite 12
Des Moines, IA 50309
(515) 243-6239
http://www.childrenscancerprograms.org

Kansas
Camp Hope
1315 SW Arrowhead Road
Topeka, KS 66604
(913) 273-4114
http://www.cancer.org/docroot/COM/content/
    div_Heartland/COM_5_1x_Camp_Hope.asp

Kentucky
The Center for Courageous Kids
1501 Burnley Road
Scottsville, KY 42164
(270) 618-2900
http://www.courageouskids.org

Home of the Innocents
1100 East Market Street
Louisville, KY 40206
(502) 596-1029
http://www.homeoftheinnocents.org

Louisiana
Camp Challenge
P.O. Box 10591
New Orleans, LA 70181
(504) 347-CAMP
http://www.campchallenge.org/

Volunteer Louisiana
620 Florida Street, Suite 210
Baton Rouge, LA 70801
(225) 342-2038
http://www.volunteerlouisiana.gov/

Maine
Maine Center on Deafness
68 Bishop Street, Suite 3
Portland, ME 04103
(800) 639-3884 (V/TTY, Toll-free)
http://www.mcdmaine.org/

Volunteer Maine
The Maine Commission for Community Service
State Planning Office
184 State Street
38 State House Station
Augusta, ME 04333
(207) 287-8933
http://www.volunteermaine.org/

Maryland
Volunteer Maryland
301 W. Preston Street, 15th Floor
Baltimore, MD 212101
(410) 767-6203
http://www.volunteermaryland.org/

Massachusetts
Coastline Elderly Services
1646 Purchase Street
New Bedford, MA 02740
(508) 999-6400
http://coastlineelderly.org/

Crossroads Family Shelter
56 Havre Street
East Boston, MA 02128
(617) 567-5926
http://www.ebcrossroads.org/

Michigan
Camp Casey
P.O. Box 2225
Birmingham, MI 48012
(248) 705-2780
http://www.camp-casey.org

Volunteer Centers of Michigan
1048 Pierpont, Suite 3
Lansing, MI 48911
(517) 492-2430
(888) 393-4737 (Toll-free, in Michigan)
http://www.mivolunteers.org/

Minnesota
HandsOn Twin Cities
2021 East Hennepin Avenue, Suite 420
Minneapolis MN 55413
(612) 379-4900
http://www.handsontwincities.org/

Mississippi
EMPOWER Community Resource Center
P.O. Box 1733
136 S. Poplar Street
Greenville, MS 38702-1733
(800) 337-4852
http://www.msempower.org/

Missouri
Lutheran Family and Children's Services of
    Missouri
401 West Boulevard North
Columbia, MO 65203
(573) 815-9955
http://www.lfcsmo.org/volunteer/

Montana
Cancer Family Network of Montana
P.O. Box 6446
Bozeman, MT 59771
(406) 587-8080
http://www.cancerfamilynetwork.org/

Western Montana Volunteer Center
c/o Missoula Aging Services
337 Stephens Avenue
Missoula, MT 59801
(406) 728-7682
http://www.volunteer.umt.edu/

Nebraska
ServeNebraska
State Capitol, 6th Floor West
1445 K Street
Lincoln, NE 68509
(800) 291-8911
http://www.serve.nebraska.gov/

Nevada
Catholic Community Services
500 E. Fourth Street
Reno, NV 89512
(775) 322-7073
http://www.ccsnn.org/

Nevada Volunteers
639 Isbell Road, Suite 220
Reno, NV 89509
(775) 825-1900
http://www.nevadavolunteers.org/

New Hampshire
Volunteer New Hampshire
117 Pleasant Street
Concord, NH 03301-3852
(603) 271-7200
http://www.volunteernh.org/html/home.htm

New Jersey
Happiness Is Camping
62 Sunset Lake Road
Hardwick, NJ 07825
(718) 295-3100
http://www.happinessiscamping.org

The Seeing Eye Inc.
10 Washington Valley Road
P.O. Box 375
Morristown, NJ 07963
(973) 539-4425
http://www.seeingeye.org/

New Mexico
Open Hands
2976 Rodeo Park Dr. East
Santa Fe, NM 87505
(505) 428-2320
http://www.openhands.org/

New York
Camp Open Arms
255 Alexander Street
Rochester, NY 14607
(716) 423-9700
http://www.canceraction.org/

New York Cares
214 West 29th Street, 5th Floor
New York, NY 10001
(212) 228-5000
http://www.newyorkcares.org/

North Carolina
Family Services, Inc.
1200 S. Broad Street
Winston-Salem, NC 27101
(336) 722-8173
http://www.familyserv.org/

NC Commission on Volunteerism and
    Community Service
Office of the Governor
20312 Mail Service Center
116 West Jones Street
Raleigh, NC 27699-0312
(919) 715-3470
http://www.volunteernc.org/

North Dakota
Lutheran Social Services of North Dakota
Bismarck: (701) 223-1510
Fargo: (701) 235-7341
Grand Forks: (701) 772-7577
Minot: (701) 838-7800
Williston: (701) 774-0749
http://www.lssnd.org/

North Dakota Parks & Recreation Department
1600 E. Century Avenue, Suite 3
Bismarck, ND 58503
(701) 328-5357
http://www.parkrec.nd.gov/parks/volunteer.
    htm

Ohio
Gift of Time Ohio
P.O. Box 866
Grove City, OH 43123
(614) 875-2100
http://www.giftoftimeohio.com/

Kids 'N Kamp
3440 Olentangy River Road, Suite 103K
Columbus, OH 43202
(614) 262-2220
http://www.kidsnkamp.org

Oklahoma
The Children's Hospital at Oklahoma University
    Medical Center
1200 Everett Drive
Oklahoma City, OK 73104
(405) 271-4700
http://www.oumedicine.com/

Oregon
Camp Quality
P.O. Box 42095
Eugene, OR 97404-0571
(541) 682-5092
http://www.campqualityusa.com

Human Solutions
12350 SE Powell Boulevard
Portland, OR 97236
(503) 548-0200
http://www.humansolutions.org/

Pennsylvania
Community Action Agency
511 Welsh Street
Chester, PA 19013
(610) 874-8451
http://www.caadc.org/

The Children's Hospital of Philadelphia
34th Street and Civic Center Boulevard
Philadelphia, PA 19104
(215) 590-1000
http://www.chop.edu

Pennsylvania Parents and Caregivers Resource
    Network
P.O. Box 4336
Harrisburg, PA 17111-0336
(888) 572-7368
http://www.ppcrn.org/

Rhode Island
Camp Hope
1043 Snake Hill Road
North Scituate, RI 02857
(401) 243-2600
http://www.cancer.org/camphoperi

Hasbro Children's Hospital
593 Eddy Street
Providence, RI 02903
(401) 444-4000
http://www.lifespan.org/hch

South Carolina
Camp Happy Days and Special Times
1622 Ashley Hall Road
Charleston, SC 29407
(843) 571-4336
http://www.camphappydays.com

SCANPO: South Carolina Association of
    Nonprofit Organizations
2711 Middleburg Drive, Suite 201
Columbia, SC 29204
(803) 929-0399
http://www.scanpo.org/

South Dakota
Senior Meals
James Valley Community Center
300 West First
Mitchell, SD 57301
(605) 995-8440
http://www.cityofmitchell.org/

Tennessee
Catholic Charities of Tennessee
30 White Bridge Rd.
Nashville, TN 37205
(615) 352-3087
http://www.cctenn.org/

Saddle Up!
1549 Old Hillsboro Road
Franklin, TN 37069-9136
(615) 794-1150
http://www.saddleupnashville.org/

Texas
Periwinkle Foundation
3000 Richmond, Suite 340
Houston, TX 77098
(713) 807-0191
http://www.periwinklefoundation.org/

Volunteer Center of North Texas
2800 Live Oak Street
Dallas, TX 75204
(866) 797-8268 (Toll-free)
http://www.volunteernorthtexas.org

Utah
Family Promise of Salt Lake
P.O. Box 996
Salt Lake City, UT 84110
(801) 961-8622
http://www.fpsl.org/

Utah Commission on Volunteers
324 South State Street, Suite 500
Salt Lake City, UT 84111
(801) 538-8700
http://volunteers.utah.gov/

Vermont
Elderly Services, Inc.
112 Exchange Street
Middlebury, VT 05753
(802) 388-3983
http://www.elderlyservices.org/

Virginia
Virginia Service Volunteer Opportunities
Virginia Department of Social Services
801 E. Main Street, 15th Floor
Richmond, VA 23219-2901
(800) 638-3839
http://www.vaservice.org/

Washington
Volunteer Washington.org
Seattle Works
1625 19th Avenue
Seattle, WA 98122
(206) 324-0808
http://www.volunteerwashington.org/

West Virginia
Volunteer WV
710 Central Avenue
Charleston, WV 25302
(304) 558-0111
http://www.volunteerwv.org/

Wisconsin
Waukesha County Backpack Coalition
500 Riverview
Waukesha, WI 53188
(262) 547-7367
http://www.backpackcoalition.org

Wyoming
Serve Wyoming
229 E. 2nd Street, Suite 203
Casper, WY 82601
(866) 737-8304
http://www.servewyoming.org/

Volunteers of America/Montana and
    Wyoming
1309 Coffeen Ave, Suite A
Sheridan, WY 82801
(307) 672-0475
http://www.voawymt.org/

Further Reading

Books

Currie-McGhee, L. K. *Miley Cyrus*. Farmington Hills, MI: Lucent Books, 2009.

Ditchfield, Christin. *Bono*. Ann Arbor, MI: Cherry Lake Publishers, 2008.

Edwards, Laurie J. *Rihanna*. Detroit: Lucent Books, 2009.

Jessup, Dallas. *Young Revolutionaries Who Rock: An Insider's Guide to Saving the World One Revolution at a Time*. Portland, OR: Sutton Hart Press, 2009.

Lesinski, Jeanne M. *Bill Gates: Entrepreneur and Philanthropist*. Minneapolis: Twenty-first Century Books, 2009.

Maxwell, Christine Reyna. *The Ultimate Volunteer Guidebook for Young People*. Yardley: Westholme, 2008.

Rubel, David. *If I Had a Hammer: Building Homes and Hope with Habitat for Humanity*. Somerville, MA: Candlewick Press, 2009.

Weatherford, Carole Boston. *Obama: Only in America*. New York: Marshall Cavendish, 2010.

Webster, Christine. *The Jonas Brothers*. New York: Weigl Publishers Inc., 2010.

Works Consulted

Agness, Phyllis J. *No Place at the Table: America's Homeless Children*. Fort Wayne, IN: Self-published, 2008.

Bartiromo, Maria. "Melinda and Bill Gates on Making a Difference," *BusinessWeek,* February 5, 2009. http://www.businessweek.com/magazine/content/09_07/b4119021540910.htm

Brinker, Nancy. "Debating Mammograms." *Newsweek,* Vol. 154, Issue 25, December 21, 2009.

Falsani, Cathleen, and Mark Allan Powell. "Bono's American Prayer." *Christianity Today,* March 2003.

Gates, William, III. "Software Breakthroughs: Solving the Toughest Problems in Computer Science." February 26, 2004. http://mitworld.mit.edu/video/209

Kelley, Kitty. *Oprah: A Biography*. New York: Crown Publishers, 2010.

"Miley Gives Back." *People, Miley Cyrus Special Issue,* Vol. 70, August 8, 2008.

On the Internet

Look to the Stars: The World of Celebrity Giving
http://www.looktothestars.org/

Reader's Digest: "10 Celebrities Who Are Giving Back"
http://www.rd.com/your-america-inspiring-people-and-stories/10-celebrities-give-back/article104702.html

World Volunteer Web
http://www.worldvolunteerweb.org/http://thedealwithdisability.blogspot.com/

Index

Kayleen Reusser, of Indiana, has written several children's books for Mitchell Lane Publishers, including *Recipe and Craft Guide to Indonesia*, Blue Banner Biographies on Taylor Swift, Selena Gomez, and Leona Lewis, and books about the Greek gods. In 2008, she began Stitches of Hope, a charity to provide free caps to people who have lost hair from illness. You can learn more about Stitches of Hope at http://www.stitchesofhope1.blogspot.com/.

DATE DUE
